Our Indian Heritage

Our Indian

by Clara Lee Tanner and Richard Kirk

Educational Consultant: LEO FAY, Professor of Education, Indiana University

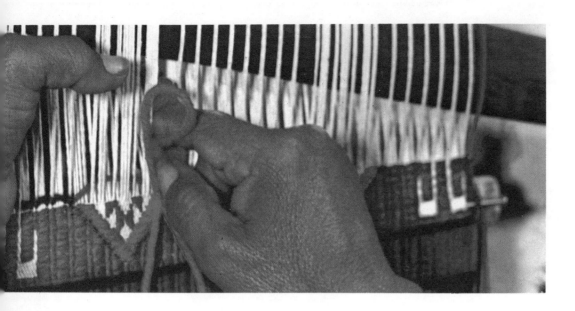

Heritage *arts that live today*

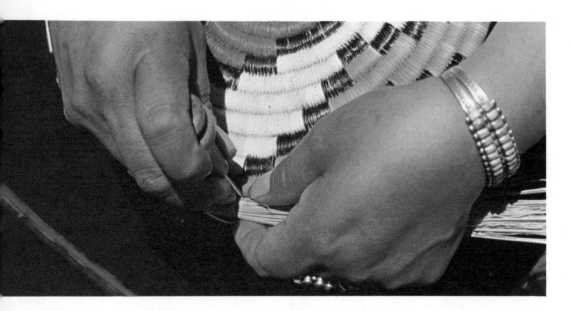

Follett Publishing Company • Chicago

Copyright © 1961 by the David-Stewart Publishing Co. • Printed in the United States of America
Library of Congress Catalog Card Number: 61-16770

Part 1 This Navajo family lives in the Southwest. The Navajos are famous for their skill in weaving beautiful blankets and rugs.

But there are many other tribes in the Southwest, and many other skills. The ancestors of today's Indians lived here and developed their crafts years and years ago.

Long before cloth weaving and basket weaving began, even before history began, there were primitive men living in the Southwest. But the land was different than it is now. There was much water in some places, and the water made plants grow that the people could use for food.

But not all people lived near the water and the plants. Those who did not were hunters. They hunted wild animals for food.

Life was so hard for these early people that it was difficult for them to stay alive. They spent most of their time looking for food. It was the problem of getting enough to eat that caused them to develop the first crafts. They needed better ways to get and prepare food.

The people who lived near the water, where plants grew in great number, shaped stones to grind the grains and leaves of the plants to make them better to eat. The hunters learned to make spears and stone knives. The spears helped them kill the animals, and the knives helped them prepare the meat and scrape the skins, for the skin was made into clothing.

Later on, weapons like the bow and arrow and the rabbit stick were invented. But it took more intelligent people to develop them.

So knives, spears and grinding stones were the first items of craft. And these early craftsmen did not create them because they wanted to make something beautiful. They made them because they needed weapons and tools to stay alive.

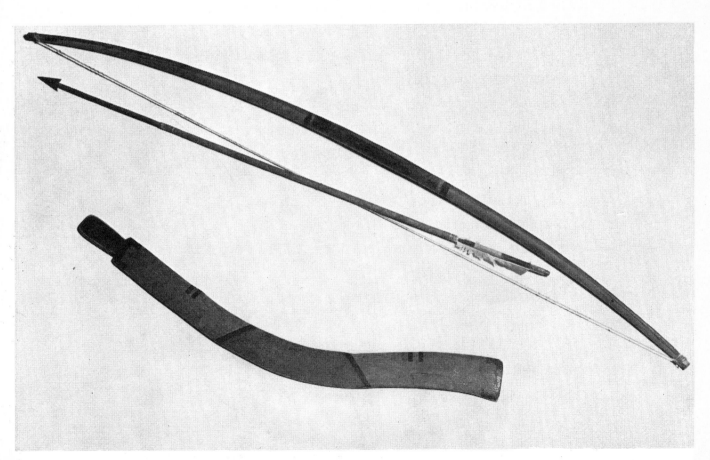

An Apache bow and arrow and a Hopi rabbit stick. The rabbit stick is used like a boomerang.

Near the beginning of the Christian era, a new group of people came to the Southwest. They settled in the north. No one knows where they lived before they arrived in the Southwest, but it is well known that they brought a new craft with them.

This skill was weaving. Because of their talent in basket weaving, they are known as the Basket Makers. Besides baskets, they could weave sandals, bags and trays. Eventually, they learned to make pottery, too. They became the masters of the Southwest.

The Basket Makers made weapons, too. They had spears and bows and arrows. They also learned to plant and cultivate crops. But while the Basket Makers were talented in many ways, they were not skilled at house making. They lived in stone-lined pits covered with brush and earth.

Later, people would come to the Southwest who could build houses, and whole villages, of stone. These stone villages, or pueblos, were the finest of the building crafts developed by the early Southwestern peoples.

Pueblo dwellers built structures like this.

The Basket Makers lived in the land for five hundred years, and then came a new group of people.

The new people knew how to weave not only baskets, but also cloth from wild cotton. It was this group that developed the pueblos. From the pueblo dwellers of this early time descended the modern pueblo-dwelling tribes like the Hopi.

In the area southwest of the pueblo dwellers, a second group arrived. They were the ancestors of tribes like the Papago. They were especially skilled in basket making and farming. This group lived

A Papago basket maker.

in square huts made of poles and earth, and they formed villages surrounded by walls of adobe, or bricks shaped from the desert clay. Of all the early people, these ancestors of the Pima and Papago and other farming tribes were the real masters of irrigation. They grew crops even in the desert.

Since the farming group made walls around their village from desert clay, they soon learned to shape the clay into pottery, too. Almost all the early people learned to make containers from the fine, desert clay.

The third important group to enter the Southwest were the ancestors of the Navajo and other wandering tribes. Part of this group had been buffalo hunters on the Great Plains, and others had lived in the cooler region to the north. They joined forces and entered the Southwest around the year 1300. Because they were nomads, or wanderers, this group had their own special crafts. They had

Pictures made by prehistoric man.

special houses, too. They lived in temporary homes made of wood and mud. These shelters are called hogans, and the Navajos still use the same kind of house.

The nomad group was hostile to the pueblo dwellers, and so the pueblo people built their stone villages high on the sides of cliffs. They could defend themselves more easily from their lofty perches.

There are many ruins in the Southwest that show the fine craftsmanship of the cliff-dwelling pueblo people.

As time went on, the crafts and skills of all three groups improved. They learned how to irrigate and cultivate crops better, or they learned how to make better weapons. Their lives became easier. They did not have to spend all their time getting food, as the earliest people had, and so they found new things to do with their extra time.

Some worked at carving pictures in stone. They made pictures of things that were

Coiled weaving done by an Apache woman.

important to them. They made pictures of the animals they hunted, or pictures of human figures. This was the beginning of art in the Southwest. Now the people wanted to make things that were not only useful, but beautiful, too.

When they made baskets, they were no longer satisfied to make a simple container. They discovered special weaves. With these, they could make baskets that had beautiful designs. These early people were like all early people. When they had time, they wanted to make something beautiful.

The pueblo-dwelling cloth weavers invented new weaves for their craft, too. Tapestry, brocade, embroidery, gauze and weft-wrapped techniques were developed by them. And these special designs are still used today. Their looms are still used by modern Indians, too. Both the upright and horizontal kinds are still seen, but the upright is used much more often.

Once art entered the lives of the people, their pottery also changed. They began to decorate their bowls and jars. They used many colors and painted a variety of subjects on their simple containers. They painted animals, people and many different designs.

Those of the early people who lived near the sea began to use colored sea shells in their crafts. They made things that were simply for decoration. This was the first jewelry. They made bracelets, armlets, beads and pendants decorated with shells or fragments of shells.

Other groups made other things to be worn just for their beauty. Stone, clay and feathers were used to make jewelry, and they often used pieces of the blue turquoise that is found in the Southwest.

But the crafts of the early people

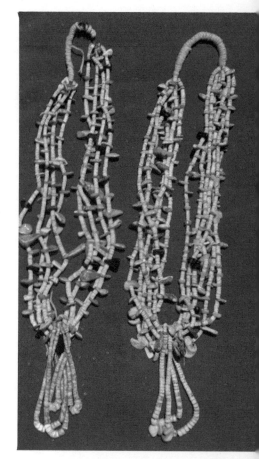

Navajo bead necklaces with turquoise and coral.

Decorated drum and rattle used in Hopi religious ceremonies.

were developed most fully in the things they made for their religious ceremonies. They had beautifully carved and painted altars. They made elaborate bowls, drums, staffs and rattles. The pueblo dwellers, who had ceremonial rooms called kivas, painted beautiful pictures on the walls showing costumed dancers and many of the special objects used in their religious rites.

In time, each of the three early groups divided into tribes. Each tribe developed its own crafts and its own special ways of living. One thing did not change, though—houses. The pueblo dwellers, the nomads and the village farmers each continued to live in the same sort of house their ancestors had.

Then, in the year 1540, the Spanish came to explore the Southwest.

Part 2 When the Spaniards came, they found the tribes divided much as they are today. The Spaniards brought with them many things the Indians had not seen before. As they moved in from the south, they bartered and traded with the tribes.

The lives and crafts of the Hopi, Zuni and Taos tribes were changed by their contact with the Span-

Hopi basket weaver.

Havasupai weaver.

ish explorers. The Havasupai, Yavapai, Maricopa, Cocopa, Apache and Navajo tribes were changed in some ways, too.

The Spaniards provided the Indians with new plants and trees—wheat, barley, melon and pepper plants and fruit trees. Some tribes found the new plants very useful, and still grow them today.

The Indians also got new animals from the explorers. Sheep, goats, donkeys, horses and cattle were among the animals the tribes obtained.

More important, the Indians traded with the Spaniards for such things as nails, majolica—a kind of pottery—horse gear and clothing. They copied these new articles and materials, or used them in their crafts. In this way especially the Indian crafts were changed.

No tribe escaped. Like the others, the Pima, Papago, Walapai, Mohave and Yuma tribes were changed by contact with the Spaniards.

The Indian's life and craft are as they are today partly because the Spanish once came to the Southwest. There are always changes when one group of people introduces its way of life to another group. But the changes caused by the Spanish were small compared to the changes caused by the next people who came.

Pima basket maker.

Yavapai woman with woven waterproof basket.

In the 1800's, the English-speaking settlers began to arrive in the Southwest. They came by way of New Mexico, meeting the eastern tribes first. They, too, bartered and traded with the Indians.

But things were not always peaceful between the Indians and the settlers. The Indians had owned the great, wild Southwest for centuries.

Sometimes they rebelled against the settlers. But the new Americans were determined to stay. And eventually, of course, they created a new nation.

Finally, the Indians were given certain territories to live in. The tracts of land reserved for them were called reservations. Many Indians still live on reservations, keeping alive their crafts and way of life.

The Indian crafts have been changed, but they are still the crafts of the original Americans. They are a proud heritage.

Sun Dance Rug, pottery and basket.

Part 3 Basket making is the oldest of the crafts. It is called "mother of the craft arts." It is called "mother" because it was first and also because it was the example for forms and designs in later crafts, like pottery.

Basketry is simply the intertwining of coarse plant materials. The leaves and stems of many kinds of plants have been used to make baskets. Bear grass, willow, cottonwood, devil's claw and rabbit brush are used, and the yucca plant is a favorite, too.

There are many ways of weaving baskets. Coiling is done by sewing strips of plant leaf over stiff foundation hoops. Usually the sewing is in small, tight weaves. When the weaves are far apart, it is called open coil.

In plaiting, the weaver crosses broad, flat strips over each other at right angles. When plaiting is more complicated, such as crossing over three

Above—Hopi baskets.
Right—Apache baskets.

Left—Hopi bread tray with plaited center. On tray is a small Hualapai storage basket. Top—Havasupai burden basket. Bottom — Chemehuevi coiled tray basket. Right — Twined Paiute water bottle.

strips and under three strips, it is called twill plaiting.

There is another method called twining. It is something like coiling, but the materials are more rigid and more varieties are used in making a single basket.

There are many kinds of baskets. Some are waterproofed to hold liquids. Others are made to carry heavy burdens on the head. Many more baskets, of all sizes and shapes, are used to hold food.

The beautiful designs in Indian baskets are made either by dyeing the materials or by using different colored plants in weaving.

Among the modern tribes, the Hopi excel at basket weaving.

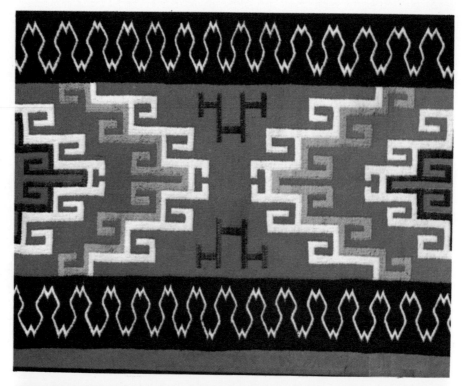

Navajo rug designs.

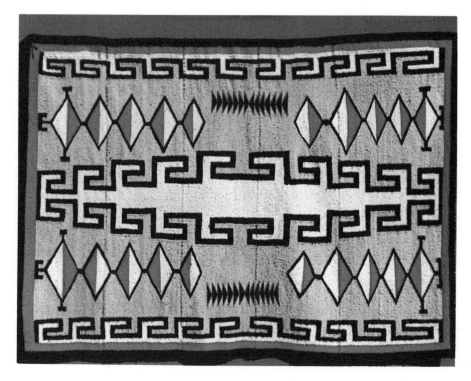

An intricate Navajo creation.

Among the tribes well known for their cloth weaving, the Navajo and Hopi are outstanding today. The Navajo were not always weavers, though. They borrowed the craft from the pueblo-dwelling Indians sometime after the Spaniards came.

There are many methods of weaving and decorating cloth, just as there are several ways to weave and decorate baskets.

There is a weave called the plain, or basket weave. The method is just like the one used in basket making. There is also a twill weave in cloth weaving that is like the twill basket weave.

Embroidery and brocading are decorative methods. Embroidery is the addition of special material after a woven piece is finished. Brocading is the addition of special material to the basic weave.

Above—Pottery made by pueblo-dwelling Indians.

*Top—Old-style Papago jar. Others, left to right—
Oval Papago jar, Maricopa two-necked jar, Pima
dish with life figures, tall-necked Maricopa vase.*

Once there were many pottery makers among the Indian tribes. The Pima and Papago women inherited the craft from their ancestors, as did many others. But they have practiced the craft less and less in modern times.

The Maricopa and Hopi tribes still make fine pottery, both for their own use and to sell to others. The Navajo make some pottery, but it is mostly decorated work to sell to tourists.

Making a good piece of pottery is difficult. First, the potter must find good clay. Adobe clay, which is used for building, does not make good pottery. It cracks too easily.

The potter must pound the clay, remove the rocks and unwanted lumps and then grind it. After that, he must sift out the finest particles. To this, he adds sand to give the sifted clay more strength. Then he slowly adds water to the mixture until it becomes doughy.

By adding roll after roll of the prepared clay, the potter builds up a foundation. Then, holding a piece of gourd rind on the outside and his hand on the inside, the potter curves the walls of the pot into the desired shape. Some tribes use a stone on the inside and a wooden paddle on the outside.

After it is shaped, the vessel must dry in the shade for a day or two before the painted decorations can be put on. After painting the object, the potter prepares a stone-lined pit to fire, or bake, the formed piece.

After a day of baking and a day of cooling, the pieces are ready for use.

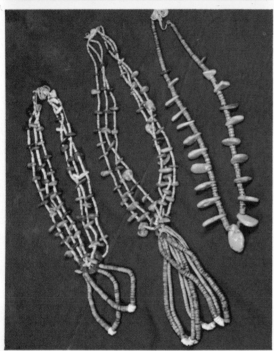

Indian jewelry making has been important through the centuries. Today, the Indian craftsmen of many tribes make necklaces, rings, pins, buckles, earrings, beaded bags and collars, and many other decorative things.

Among the earliest decorations were sea shells and the beautiful blue turquoise of the Southwestern desert. Disc bands of shell with chunks of turquoise still make one of the most popular necklaces of the Hopi and Navajo tribes. Today, the Navajo and the pueblo-dwelling tribes wear more jewelry than do most of the others.

Coral arrived in the Southwest in the eighteenth century. It was brought in by traders. Because it was so gem-like, it quickly became popular with many of the Indian tribes.

Coral is still used to make many pieces of jewelry. A Navajo craftsman will spend hours trying to match strings of coral.

Top—Bead articles by Apaches.
Center—Navajo bead necklaces.
Bottom—Apache beaded bags.

As in all crafts, the arrival of new people in the land of the Indians caused changes in their jewelry.

Bringing in coral made one important change, for coral is from the sea and must be imported for the Indian craftsmen. If explorers and settlers had not gone into the Southwest, the Indians would never have seen this beautiful material.

It is well known that the English-speaking settlers brought glass beads to trade with the Indian tribes.

The Apaches and Utes were quick to use these new, shiny decorations. And the Navajo have used them a great deal, too.

The Mohave and Yuma tribes are known for their fine, beaded collars. The collars are made in many colors and in many beautiful designs. Most of them are used for religious ceremonies and other special occasions that are important in the Indian way of life.

But it was silver that brought about the greatest changes in the Indian crafts. The new material was introduced to the Indian tribes soon after 1850. The Navajos liked the silvery metal immediately and have used it ever since to make jewelry.

The Hopi, too, have developed a great fondness for silver, and they have made excellent pieces of jewelry with it.

Zuni jewelry made from silver is outstanding. Their pieces have great precision.

Of all the items of Indian craft, jewelry made by Indian silversmiths is probably the most popular with collectors.

The crafts and the way of life of all Indians are still changing.

Many Indians no longer dress in their traditional tribal clothing, although a few still cling to the older kind of dress. But most Indians have kept alive the tradition of ceremonial clothing, which is still woven of cotton on the ancient looms.

The Indians no longer make many things which they once needed for their own use, like cooking pots and other items of everyday life. They can now buy many of these things in stores more easily than they can make them.

Much that the Indians make today is sold to other Americans who like to collect original items of Indian craftsmanship. This has caused changes in the crafts.

Many things that Indians would not have made for their own use, they now make for selling to collectors. And, of course, they make much that is sold as souvenirs to tourists.

Top—Zuni necklace.
Center—Zuni bracelets.
Bottom—Various Zuni pieces.

There are not so many Indian craftsmen as there used to be. Indian children, when they are grown, often find jobs or go to schools in other parts of America. So there are fewer and fewer new craftsmen to carry on the ancient skills.

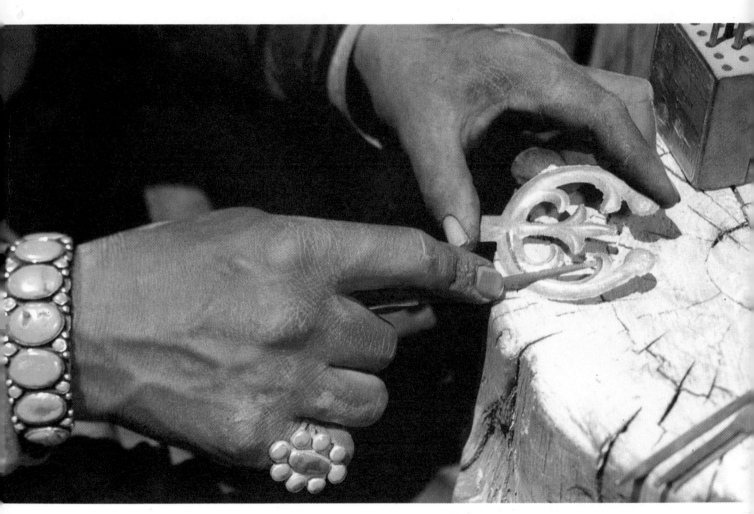

Hands of a Navajo silversmith.

But there are still many talented hands, still many nimble fingers to produce fine and unique items. And there will be outstanding Indian craftsmen for many years to come.

GLOSSARY

Key to Pronunciation of Vowels:

a	pat, lap	ėr	her, learn	oi	boil, choice	ə represents any vowel in
ā	ate, tale	i	lid, pit	ou	our, mouse	an unaccented syllable:
ã	bare, stair	ī	mine, kite	u	cut, supper	a in along, e in broken,
ä	car, father	o	cot, hop	ū	use, few	i in pencil, o in melon,
e	red, step	ō	tone, blow	u̇	put, wool	u in suppose
ē	sleep, me	ô	border, fall	ü	rule, school	

A heavy mark (′) follows the most strongly accented or stressed syllable in a word (ban′ish); a lighter mark (′) follows a syllable on which there is some stress, usually in a word of many syllables (pär tis′ə pa′shən).

adobe (ə dō′bi), brick made of earth or clay dried in the sun.

ancestor (an′ ses tər), a person from whom one is directly descended, such as a grandparent.

armlet (ärm′lət), a bracelet or band for the upper arm.

barter (bär′tər), to trade one thing for another without using money.

ceremony (ser′ ə mō′ni), an act or series of acts performed in a regular order as required by law or custom.

coral (kôr′ əl), a stony material composed of the skeletons of tiny sea creatures, much used in making jewelry.

craft (kraft), skill; art or trade requiring skill.

disc (disk), a flat, thin, round piece of metal or other material, like a plate or coin.

dye (dī), a coloring substance used to stain cloth or other materials.

gear (gēr), part of the harness of a horse.

hogan (hō′ gan), an earth-covered dwelling of the Navajo Indians.

kiva (kē′və), a special inner room in a pueblo, used for religious ceremonies.

loom (lüm), a frame or machine for weaving yarn or threads into cloth.

majolica (mə jol′ i kə), a kind of highly colored pottery with a glassy finish.

nomad (nō′mad), one of a tribe which has no fixed home but wanders from place to place.

pendant (pen′ dənt), a hanging ornament, as an earring or locket.

pottery (pot′ ər i), pots, dishes and vases made from clay; the place where such articles are made. The person who makes these things is a potter.

pueblo (pweb′ lō), one of the Indian villages in the Southwest, built of adobe or stone.

reservation (rez′ ər vā′ shən), an area of public land set aside or reserved for Indians to live on.

rigid (rij′ id), stiff, unbending.

rind (rīnd), the outer peel of a fruit or vegetable.

staff (staf), a pole, stick or rod, used to support or hold up something.

turquoise (ter′ koiz), a blue or blue-green stone used as a gem.

waterproof (wô′ tər prüf), not letting water through, as a waterproof material.

Grateful credit is given to *Arizona Highways*, its editor, Raymond Carlson, and its staff for their assistance in producing *Our Indian Heritage: Arts That Live Today;* to Ted De Grazia for the drawings which appear on pages 1, 6, 8, 11 and 15; to Earl Hammock for the painting on page 21; to *Western Ways* for the photograph on page 10; and to the following photographers whose work appears in the book: Chuck Abbott, page 9; Martha Burleigh, 2 (top); Roy L. Caples, 31; Ray Manley, 2 (bottom), 3 (bottom), 7, 15, 16, 23, 26 (bottom); J. H. McGibbeny, back cover, 3 (top), 14; Josef Muench, 4-5, 22 (right), 24, 25, 26 (top), 28; Tad Nichols, 30; R. H. Peebles, 12, 18, 19, 20, 22 (left); Allen C. Reed, front cover; E. T. Scoyen, 13; and Bob Towers, 17.